Book 2 in the Land t

Activating Your Fortune

IMPLEMENTING YOUR BIGGER FUTURE

A Step-by-Step Guide for Leveraging The Launch Sequence®
in Your Next Master Planned Community

Other Books by Carter Froelich

The Real Estate Wake Up Call:
The Secrets to Real Estate Success

Land to Lots:
How to Borrow Money You Don't Have to Pay Back
and LAUNCH Master Planned Communities

Fields to Fortune: Planning Your Bigger Future

Book 2 in the Land to Lots® Trilogy

Activating Your Fortune

IMPLEMENTING YOUR BIGGER FUTURE

A Step-by-Step Guide for Leveraging The Launch Sequence®
in Your Next Master Planned Community

CARTER FROELICH

ethos
collective

Printed in the United States of America

Published by Igniting Souls
PO Box 43, Powell, OH 43065
IgnitingSouls.com

LCCN: 2024925190

Paperback ISBN: 978-1-63680-433-0

Hardback ISBN: 978-1-63680-434-7

eBook ISBN: 978-1-63680-435-4

Available in paperback, hardcover, e-book, and audiobook.

To the visionaries and pioneers in the development industry who strive to transform ideas into reality, and to the teams who execute with precision and dedication. May this book inspire innovation, collaboration, and success in your projects.

Contents

Introduction 11

    What is The Launch Sequence˚? 12

    Why Should I Care? 13

Part 1—Cross-Check

Why Implementation? 19

The Project Financing Checklist™ 25

Part 2—Countdown

Add Favorable Financing Language
    to the Development Agreement 33

        Special District Issues to Consider 38

        Performing the RED Analysis™ 45

        Financing Other Costs 48

Prepare the District Petition and
  Formation Application 55
Coordinate the District Formation Process 59
Review the Assessment Methodology
  (If Applicable) 61
Review Appraisal and Market Study 64
Request Bond Issuance and Assist in the
  Preparation of the Official Statement. 67
Review the Bond Documents for
  Clarity of Financial Matters 72

Part 3—Lift Off

Next Steps 77
Afterword. 79
About the Author. 83

Scan the QR Code below to Access Supplemental Documents and Book Bonuses

Introduction

This is the second installment of the Land to Lots®
Trilogy, a value enhancement series with all the
information you need to take your master planned
community from start to finish. By reading this book,
you have entered the middle of a journey from land to
lots and from fields to fortune. As your guide on this
journey, I offer you the expertise of over forty years
of helping people like you achieve their land development goals. My team at Launch Development
Finance Advisors works with land developers, com-
mercial developers, and home builders to finance
their infrastructure using a proven process called The
Launch Sequence®. Before we dive in, let's review The
Launch Sequence process as a whole and assess how
far we have already come.

What is The Launch Sequence®?

The Launch Sequence is a unique process we at Launch Development Finance Advisors have developed by working with land developers and home builders around the United States for over forty years. In assisting them with finance and public infrastructure through a myriad of different means, we have perfected our processes and created an infinitely applicable land development value-enhancement process that assists our clients in financing public infrastructure with long-term (twenty-five-plus year) non-recourse, tax-exempt bonds, reduce costs, and mitigate risks, all with the goal of enhancing project profitability and returns.

The genius of The Launch Sequence is it enables our clients to borrow money to finance infrastructure in such a way that the end users of the project pay it back. In essence, you get to borrow money you don't have to repay.

It almost sounds too good to be true, doesn't it?

But the truth is, The Launch Sequence works every time, all the time. It works on big projects. It works on small projects. It works in every state and every situation. The Launch Sequence is a flexible formula, but it is also a living process, and both factors contribute to its enduring success.

Every time we have a "learning experience," whether good or bad, we incorporate it into The Launch Sequence. We use several tools to memorialize and universalize our experiences, but regardless of the situation, we learn and grow from each of our thousands of transactions so our clients can benefit.

So, how does it work? Fundamentally, every developer starts with a jigsaw puzzle box. Inside are their goals, challenges, and opportunities, but they are all puzzle pieces jumbled together. We take that box and dump it out on the table. From there, it's just a matter of sorting the puzzle pieces by color, shape, and image as we get a feel for the size and possibility of the project. In other words, we find out where the client wants to go and what tools we have at our disposal based on the specific state and jurisdiction to help our client complete their vision.

The Launch Sequence has three stages: the Planning Process, the Implementation Process, and the Management Process. *Fields to Fortune: Planning Your Bigger Future* is the first book in this series, and it covers the Planning Process in detail. If you have not read it, I highly recommend picking that up first. It gives you every tool necessary to formulate an adaptive project plan. This book turns to the Implementation Process, where we take the plans we've created and implement them. Now is the time to take your land development project from ideas to reality.

Why Should I Care?

The alternative to The Launch Sequence is simply hiring an underwriter to do your Special District (e.g., CFD, CDD, Metro, MUD, SID, PID, etc.) bond sizing and be done with it. I mentioned this in *Fields to*

Fortune, and I will repeat it here: I have great admiration and affection for my underwriting colleagues. There is no question that they are very good at what they do.

It is important to remember, however, that underwriters don't work for you. Yes, the underwriters are the ones who issue the bonds and secure the money, and ultimately, that is the goal of any type of Special District financing. Nonetheless, the two perspectives differ in that the underwriters typically work first for the bond buyers, then for the district or jurisdiction, and only lastly for the developer. They will necessarily see things from the perspective of issuing the largest bond possible (as they are paid based upon the par amount of the bonds) and of doing so in the shortest time possible with a bond structure that allows them the easiest and fastest marketing and sales period.

As such, these goals can and do often ignore the realities of:

- Developing a master planned community
- Changing real estate market conditions
- Total effective property tax rate considerations
- Construction phasing
- Development impact fee credits
- Other benefiting land owners
- Oversizing requirements
- Other reimbursement mechanisms

- The developer's Project Vision™
- The Return Factor Question™
- Financing goals
- Business plan

Since I began providing professional advisory services to the private sector in the mid-1980s, I have had one driving interest—that of my private sector developer clients. Neither I nor the Launch Development Financing Advisor (Launch) professionals work for underwriters, financial advisors, districts, or the public sector. Our only focus is helping our private sector development clients achieve their vision and business plan. When we implement The Launch Sequence, we genuinely want the best for our clients.

Underwriters and financial advisors rarely have the experience we do when working across the entirety of a project. We consider first and foremost what our clients want to achieve and how they will judge their financial success. We then lay out detailed plans to achieve these goals. We take a much broader view of what we can do for our clients to help them finance infrastructure, reduce costs, and mitigate risks, all with the goal of enhancing project profitability.

Throughout this exposition of the Implementation Process, you will see many lists of questions. Use these as a guide to start personalizing The Launch Sequence to your unique needs. We can provide structure and a method, but nothing will take flight until the details of *your* project are on the launch pad.

PART 1
Cross-Check

Why Implementation?

Simply put, the Implementation Process is the execution of the Launch Finance Plan we developed during the Planning Process. As a reminder, the Planning Process always begins by taking our clients through an interview where they describe their Project Vision as precisely as possible.

During this discovery phase, we conduct a version of Dan Sullivan's D.O.S. Conversation® from the Strategic Coach® Program. D.O.S. stands for Dangers, Opportunities, and Strengths. By organizing project information into these categories for our client, we have a good idea of where we need to spend extra time and attention to make sure our client's potential roadblocks can be overcome, their opportunities captured, and their project and company strengths leveraged.

During the Planning Phase, we also have our clients answer the Return Factor Question, which identifies the financial metric our client prefers to use to judge their financial performance. Are they driven by the internal rate of return (IRR) or by nominal dollars (e.g., multiple)? Most of our clients say they want both; however, we ask that they only select one response because the answer to this question will set the stage for the selection of the financing vehicle(s) to be used in the project financing and inform us as to what will need to be included in legal agreements with the jurisdiction, agencies, and Special Districts.

I can't emphasize enough the importance of Project Vision, D.O.S. Conversation, and the Return Factor Question. The response to these questions is where the financial destination of the Project is laid out. Without this destination in mind, we cannot begin to handcraft the detailed Project Path and Plan™ for our client. The Project Path and Plan is the blueprint document we prepare that enumerates all of the financing vehicles we want to include in our project financing as well as all of the specific deal points we will need to include in the entitlement or financing agreements that will be in place during the duration of the project's buildout.

This document is curated to the specific needs of the client based on their goals and objectives. It is handcrafted to ensure it will provide certainty as to what financing tools will be available during the buildout of the project but will also create flexibility for the client to be able to adapt to changes in the local real estate market.

The high-level concepts contained within the Project Path and Plan are then simplified and included in The Launch Finance Plan, which is presented to the decision makers (e.g., jurisdictional councils and staff) for their consideration and feedback. The presentation of the Finance Plan and the responses provided by the jurisdictional representatives provide the client with clarity as to what the jurisdiction is willing to assist our clients with as part of the financing, what they will not do, and what they may request in return.

With this real-time feedback from the jurisdictional representatives, we generally know with approximately eighty percent certainty the elements of the Finance Plan we can count on. We can determine the financial impacts of any negotiation items brought up during the presentation of the Finance Plan that will have to be negotiated during the Implementation Phase of The Launch Sequence.

This represents the culmination of the Planning Phase of The Launch Sequence. It's now time for action and implementation.

At this point, you may be wondering why the Implementation Process requires its own separate stage of The Launch Sequence. Especially if you have taken the time to secure a detailed and carefully constructed plan, you might think you can breeze through the rest of the project without issues.

Mike Tyson once said something along the lines of, "Everyone has a plan until they get punched in the face." The Implementation Process is where we at Launch work with our clients to make sure they don't get punched in the face.

I have seen so many projects where what was originally planned and agreed to was not what was reflected in the legal and financing documents. One punch in the face, one miscommunication or misrepresentation, and all your careful planning goes down the drain.

Many of the issues created in the implementation of the project financing arise when the jurisdiction begins to bring on outside legal counsel and financial advisors to assist them with the documentation required to set up the financing vehicles and concepts laid out in the Finance Plan. These consultants were typically not in the transaction when the Finance Plan was presented. Instead, they were "told" what the deal was by the jurisdiction, and the game of telephone began.

Many of these consultants believe they can merely take the last deal they did, which "kind-of-sort-of" matches the transaction structure they were "told" about, and cut and paste these documents for the transaction. This can't ever work, as every one of the transactions we prepare for our clients is handcrafted for the specific D.O.S. of the project and the client. As such, there are no "off-the-shelf" documents that will memorialize the intricacies of the proposed transaction.

Every client's situation is different, and to respect that fact, we custom-craft every transaction specifically for the client. These are bespoke financing structures, and as such, no baseline agreements exist or will suffice. So, when I say we help you implement your plan, that is precisely what I mean. Not just any plan; *your* plan. Whatever the jurisdiction approves, we ensure that the exact mandate is implemented.

Over the years of working with various attorneys and underwriters, I've seen absurd mistakes. Sometimes, the baseline legal and financing agreements show different cities. If the attorneys can't even do a simple search and replace on their legal agreements, how can we expect them to outline detailed financing concepts specific to the project and our client?

I've seen underwriters write on the official statement of the bond offering that the bond issuance is a taxable bond when it is, in fact, a tax-exempt bond. Sometimes, even the developer's name is wrong. And these are the easy details!

The hard part is documenting and implementing the actual financing and structure of the project, and I can guarantee if the easy stuff is wrong, the hard, detailed stuff will not be accurate either. Our priority at Launch is to be the Air Traffic Control during any transaction—we watch over all consultants, attorneys, and underwriters while making sure everything goes to plan without unnecessary collisions.

This is the sole purpose of the Implementation Phase—to ensure that everything the developer planned is implemented. If the underlying legal documents do not clearly outline the proposed transaction in such a fashion that a monkey could read and understand the transaction, the client is at risk. At any point down the line, a new jurisdictional council or staff member can start reading things into the financing documents that are not there or weren't intended by the parties at the time the financing was planned and documented.

Takeaway: You may have the best financing plan ever made for your master planned community, but if you do not handle the Implementation Process with the same precision, it could still fall to pieces.

The Project Financing Checklist™

Our solution for transitioning between planning and implementation is what we call a Project Financing Checklist™. The Project Financing Checklist is a more detailed list of every important element of the plan as originally outlined in the Project Path and Plan and the Finance Plan. This is the list of items to be considered as the project moves forward and activates.

The checklist is an organic, living document. It lays out the project's specific deal points and includes every tip, trick, and potential pitfall that might trip up the financing we have identified over the forty-plus years we have represented the private sector. We include things that have worked and attempts that badly failed. But every learning experience, both good and bad, is on this checklist.

As you may have gathered, I love checklists. In my early career, I was an auditor at a "Big 8" accounting firm. When performing an audit, we had to follow Audit Programs and Quality Control Checklists. This is where I was initially introduced to the concepts of processes and checklists.

The encounter that forever sold me on the use of checklists was when I attended the University of Southern California (USC) in 1987 to get my Master's in Real Estate Development (MRED). At the time, USC's Developer in Residence was Ralph Lewis, the founder of Lewis Homes, which is now called the Lewis Group of Companies. Ralph also started out his career as an accountant and had a knowledge of, and an affinity for, checklists. Ralph shared with the MRED class Lewis Home's Land Buying Checklist. The checklist was broken into categories and had 347 different questions and/or action items that had to be addressed prior to the purchase of land.

I read the document and found many of the action items and questions to be things that one would normally do when purchasing land, such as confirming zoning classifications and checking the availability of utilities. Then, there were very specific questions, some of which seemed rather odd. The oddest statement that I still remember was, "If purchasing land near a crematorium, verify that human remains have not been spread on the land in question." I asked Ralph about the nature of the land buying checklist and, in particular, the crematorium question. He responded that the checklist was an accumulation of every mistake they had ever made buying land. And when a mistake was made, it was added to the land buying checklist. Ralph said, "This way, we'll never make the same mistake again."

I recently had the opportunity to interview Ralph's son Randall Lewis, who is continuing the family business along with his brothers and newer generations of the Lewis family. I asked Randall how many questions were currently on the land buying checklist. He responded with "632." This goes to show that no matter how long you have been practicing your craft, no matter how much you think you know, you will always be having new "learning experiences." I thought the land buying checklist was pure genius, and as a result, we at Launch have checklists for all of our processes so we capture our learning experiences.

Coming back to the Project Financing Checklist, the key is to have a healthy list of items we need to implement and monitor but also a list of items to make sure we avoid. Some of the categories in the Project Financing Checklist include the following:

1. Project Vision Response

2. Return Factor Question Response

3. D.O.S. Conversation Results

    a. Listing of Transformative Strategies to:

        i. Overcome Dangers

        ii. Capture Opportunities

        iii. Leverage Strengths

4. Detailed Deal Points from the Project Path and Plan and Supporting Documents/Analysis including:

   a. The Launch Competitive Tax Rate Analysis

   b. The Launch Market Driven Bond Sizing

   c. The Eligible Cost and Fee Analysis

   d. The Cost Segregation Analysis

   e. RED Analysis (Reduce Eliminate Defer)

   f. DIF Credit Analysis

   g. Oversizing Analysis

   h. Other Benefiting Landowners from Project Infrastructure

5. Jurisdictional Experiences

6. Required Legal Agreement Frameworks

7. Required Financing Frameworks

8. District Bidding and Contracting Requirements

9. Specific Language Requirements on Maps of Dedication / Plat Maps

10. Requirements for Eligible Cost Reimbursement

11. List of Launch Learning Experiences

We not only have to compile the checklist, but we also refer to it religiously. It would be counterproductive to go through with something only to find that we had missed something from the Project Financing Checklist.

If you're not working with Launch for your own project, I recommend you take the time to compile a checklist of your own using the list above as a reference tool. It pays off to stay organized. An extra checklist is an invaluable failsafe, particularly if it contains every potential and existing consideration for the implementation of your master planned community financing.

Next, we will dive into the memorialization of your Finance Plan, creating the district and issuing bonds and other related items—everything necessary for Activating your Fortune. Keep in mind that activation of a financing is not fully successful unless it is the financing we planned and presented to the jurisdictional representatives and is the plan that will help you achieve your Project Vision and return metrics.

Takeaway: Keep track of your success and "learning experiences" by including them in an organic checklist. Make sure that you and your company are capturing all of these experiences and referring to them on a regular basis.

PART 2
Countdown

Add Favorable Financing Language to the Development Agreement

Sun Tzu, the brilliant Chinese general and strategist, said, "Every battle is won before it is fought." This quote emphasizes the importance of preparation, as the extra time spent preparing leads to better outcomes and the avoidance of potential unforeseen catastrophes. In my experience, these words run no truer than taking the time to prepare a thoughtful and thorough annexation agreement (if appropriate), development agreement, entitlement, and/or other financing-related documents, collectively referred to as the Development Agreement(s).

One of the most important steps in our Planning Process was to identify the major dangers that had to be overcome and the opportunities that had to be captured in order to ensure successful project financing. As part of this stage of the Implementation Process, we are going to begin to memorialize those deal points in the Development Agreement.

This is critical because the legal documents created as part of the entitlements and financing will act as the foundation of the financing structure on which other supportive financing vehicles will be anchored. Additionally, the Development Agreement will be in existence for the life of the project, and we don't want to have to go back to the jurisdiction and ask for an amendment. If we do, in my experience, the jurisdiction will also want to add new deal points to the Development Agreement, and these changes could materially impact the performance of the project.

As such, our mantra in drafting Development Agreements is "One Time Right." I cannot tell you how important it is to have a Development Agreement either prior to or in conjunction with the establishment of your Special District. If you don't, this could come back to haunt you.

For example, I had a public builder client annexing their project into a jurisdiction, and as part of the annexation process, I was tasked with loading up their Pre-Annexation and Development Agreement (PADA) with favorable district financing language. To add further color to the background of this story, the annexation and entitlement of this project were happening during a hot market cycle, and our client was eager to get the project annexed, entitled, and developed and to begin selling houses to the seemingly endless amount of buyers in the market.

The City, also eager to streamline the process, kept on telling our client not to worry about the establishment of the Special Taxing District and to leave all of the specific financing language out of the PADA. The jurisdiction representatives assured our client that they would establish the district when asked once the property had been annexed. I advised our client to stay the course but was overruled. The favorable financing language came out of the PADA, and the property was annexed into the City.

Six months later, when my client went to the jurisdiction to request the establishment of the financing district, the jurisdiction staff indicated that they were happy to assist—with two conditions. First, the fire station our client had originally agreed to build in year seven of the project had to be constructed in year two instead. Second, my client had to agree to fund $1 million per year for five years to staff the fire station with two crews.

This was an expensive lesson for our client, and it has completely jaded me when dealing with jurisdictions. This is why I always recommend to our clients that we document the understanding of the transaction in clear, simple language and even add mathematical formulas (if necessary) to Development Agreements to make them clear, concise, understandable, repeatable, and able to stand the test of time.

On a happier note, while annexing into another City, one of our other clients stuck to their guns and loaded up their PADA with favorable financing language to allow for the establishment of multiple Special Districts, a Special District ad valorem tax rate of $10 per $100 of assessed valuation, favorable development impact fee language, and the creation of reimbursement agreements to require other benefiting landowners to fund their pro-rata share of public facilities.

During this negotiation process, the jurisdiction staff was so concerned about hillside ordinances, architectural guidelines, and product mix that they never commented on our financing language. When we annexed the property and approached the jurisdiction with our application to establish the Special District pursuant to the terms of the PADA, the jurisdiction staff indicated that they were not willing to increase the ad valorem tax rate to $10 per $100 of assessed valuation as all of the other developers in the jurisdiction had only increased their Special District ad valorem taxes by $3 per $100 of assessed valuation.

When this occurred, I indicated that the jurisdiction had already agreed to the $10 tax rate increase as part of the approval of the PADA. The jurisdiction staff was incredulous, and they immediately jumped out of their conference room chairs to retrieve a copy of the PADA.

They didn't have to go far, as I had in my possession a copy of the county-recorded PADA, and I turned to the page on which the $10 tax rate was documented.

Suffice it to say, this ended the conversation. We were allowed to go forward with the district formation and the use of the $10 tax rate. The amount of revenue the $10 tax rate was estimated to produce over time made the district financing more valuable than what the developer had paid for the land!

So why did we increase the project's tax rate by $10 when all other projects kept their tax rate increases to $3? The difference with this project was that when we were performing our Competitive Tax Rate Analysis, we noted the project was located in a school district containing a nuclear power plant. In other words, the school district had a huge assessed valuation, and thereby, the total property taxes being charged by the jurisdiction and the school district were $10 less than the competitive projects.

Therefore, we could increase our ad valorem tax rate by $10 and be at the same effective tax rate level as our competition. In my experience, home buyers purchase new homes because they love the community, the home is in a great school district, the project is close to work, or the home buyers fell in love with the kitchen.

Not to have increased the tax rate would have left tens of millions of dollars on the table without a corresponding increase in lot prices, home prices, or sales velocity. This is why we increased the property tax rate. After twenty-plus years, the master planned community has been a huge success, and we have been able to issue tens of millions of bonds through the Special District without impacting home prices or sales paces.

There's a myriad of considerations to be included in any Development Agreement. The items that the professionals at Launch are concerned with are those that were outlined when we initially met with our client when we went through the Project Vision, the DOS Conversation, and the Return Factor Question, in addition to specific infrastructure construction-related items such as the timing of construction and oversizing.

Special District Issues to Consider

As it relates to including language in the Development Agreement associated with the creation of the Special District, the most important wording focuses on the word "shall" versus the term "may." Let me explain.

Oftentimes, jurisdictions want to soften language in the Development Agreement indicating that once an application and/or petition for the creation of a Special District is received, the jurisdiction "may" take such action as required to establish the district. This is not sufficient to create the certainty we need as a developer soon to finance tens of millions of dollars of public infrastructure for the benefit of the jurisdiction.

The language we would like to include in the Development Agreement is that the jurisdiction "shall" take such action as required to establish the district. If the inclusion of this language is not possible, we strongly recommend that our clients establish the Special District in tandem with the negotiations of the Development Agreement.

From there, we also need to address anything specific to the Special District. For example, as part of the district, what are the maximum equivalent property tax rates we can bond up to?

While every item to consider when preparing a Development Agreement is specific to each project, state, and individual jurisdiction and is thus beyond the scope of this book, some of the general topics that should be covered and included in the Development Agreement are:

1. What type of Special District is being requested to be established? Note: Some states have multiple Special District options, and it's possible to indicate that at the sole discretion and request of the developer, the jurisdiction will allow the formation of any of the allowed Special Districts.

2. What types of bonds are being requested to be issued by the Special District? Again, some states and their Special District legislation allow multiple bond types to be issued. For example, in the state of Arizona, a community facilities district can issue general obligation, special assessment, and/or revenue bonds.

3. What are the public improvements the developer is requesting the jurisdiction and/or Special District to finance? Generally, you want the flexibility to finance all authorized improvements as allowed by law.

4. Ability to use the bond proceeds for both construction and reimbursement of eligible public improvements.

5. Ability to bring other benefiting landowners into the Special District boundary should they be found to benefit from the district public improvements. This is a great way to get other benefiting landowners to pay their fair share costs of the infrastructure. Other benefiting landowners can be brought into the district kicking and screaming, provided we have the majority acreage, voter, and/or assessed valuation as required by specific state statutes. Additionally, be advised that this may force the developer to spend political capital with the jurisdiction; however, if the costs are sufficient, it may be worth the cost.

6. Ad valorem target tax rates. Memorialize the target tax rate that was outlined in the Launch Competitive Tax Rate Analysis.

7. Bond Authorization amounts. Make sure you ask for the largest amount possible, factoring in home price and assessed valuation increases over the life of the project as well as construction costs increases. Remember that once you vote on a Bond Authorization amount, this figure is set in stone and cannot be changed without landowner (read "homeowner") approval.

8. Special District governance (different states offer different options. We want the Special District governance that provides the most certainty on behalf of the developer).

9. Special Assessment Value to Lien Requirements. The industry average is 3 to 1, meaning that if a lot is valued at $100,000, we can issue special assessment bonds with an average per lot lien of $33,333 ($100,000 / 3).

10. Bond Term. Again, different states offer different options. You want the longest term allowed by law.

These are just some of the items we will be documenting in the Development Agreement as they relate to the major Special District deal points.

Obviously, the developer wants to have a say in which professionals have a part in the project. Not all professionals who are selected by a jurisdiction or a district board have the right mindset to assist in the financing. Some legal and financial advisor professionals can be "deal-killers" rather than "deal-makers." We only want to work with "deal-makers." Accordingly, we want to lay out language indicating that the developer and district board will jointly select the following:

a. Underwriter

b. Bond Counsel

c. Financial Advisor

d. Assessment Engineer (special assessment bonds only)

e. Appraiser (special assessment bonds only)

f. Market Consultant

We then review our list of eligible public infrastructure we want to finance, and if there's anything that may be a little iffy given the state's Special District enabling legislation, it's important to call that out specifically.

For example, let's look at real property interests. Most state enabling legislation allows developers to finance real property interest; however, this term is not defined, and many jurisdictions don't want the developers to finance real property interests. They want the developer to finance roads, water, sewer, parks, and fire stations. We contend that without the land, easements, and rights-of-way in which these facilities are constructed, there would be no roads, water, sewer, parks, or fire stations. Therefore, we want the ability to reimburse the developer for the fair market value of these real property interests as part of the cost of the infrastructure.

Secondly, we want to make our shopping basket of eligible infrastructure as large as possible so we can determine what facilities we want to finance and when we want to finance them. Having the district acquire real property interests is a great way to accelerate cash into the project pro forma.

As a case in point, during the Great Recession, we utilized special assessment bonds to acquire the rights-of-way for a major arterial roadway that was planned to run through a dense mixed-use development project in Idaho. With the district's acquisition of the right-of-way, the developer was able to recapitalize their project and continue to move forward with additional improvements even though we were in the middle of the Great Recession. As of the date of this writing, the majority of the project is built out, and it is a jewel box in the city of Boise.

We may also want to include the developer's financing costs. In essence, we are telling the jurisdiction, "Together, we are creating this district. However, we, as the developer, are borrowing very expensive money to build the public facilities, and the Special District won't fully reimburse us for many years. As such, we want to make sure the district is reimbursing us not only for the cost of the facilities but also for the financing charges we incur." Again, we are only asking for the same treatment as the jurisdictions. When a jurisdiction finances public facilities, it gets repaid for its financing costs, which we are also asking for. All of this will go into the Development Agreement to memorialize the parties' understanding.

Other district-specific items that need to go in the Development Agreement include appraisal and assessment methodologies. If we are using assessment bonds, we outline the scope of work related to how the appraisal should be done and how specific value estimates, such as retail value, bulk wholesale value, and as-is value, should be estimated as part of the appraisal process and what value will be used by the underwriter to size the bonds. Additionally, do these values apply to finished lots, superpads, and just-plated and engineered lots? The difference between these values is dramatic and often means the difference between the project making financial sense or not.

Sometimes, jurisdictional policies require that the Special District only issue bonds in an amount equal to thirty-three percent of the as-is value of the land (i.e., three-to-one value to lien ratio). This requirement doesn't provide a lot of funding for infrastructure and does little good to move the project forward. Imagine the difference if we instead are able to borrow thirty-three percent of the value of the land, assuming the infrastructure to be financed by the bonds and any other infrastructure projects for which performance guarantees have been provided are in place as of the date of valuation (e.g., finished lot value). These appraisal assumptions are going to give us a much higher value and, therefore, many more bond proceeds to construct and/or be reimbursed for public infrastructure costs. This is why we want to add them to the Development Agreement.

Dovetailing off the discussion related to appraisal requirements, we also want to include clarity around the value-to-lien ratio. Here, we're identifying whether the ratio is three-to-one or something greater. The industry standard is three-to-one. However, we have negotiated deals in which we can issue bonds at a one-to-one value-to-lien ratio, provided our clients buy their own bonds and do not sell the bonds to the open market until the three-to-one value-to-lien ratio has been achieved.

Additionally, we want to lay out expectations as to what happens if we don't hit the required ratio. Launch's goal is to create the largest cash flow for our clients with the least costs. Therefore, rather than limiting the funds we can issue, we work into the Development Agreement several mechanisms to help us if we fall short of the stated ratio so we will not leave any money on the table. These mechanisms might include the following:

- Providing other collateral to achieve the required value-to-lien ratio (e.g., MAI appraised real estate, letters of credit, or other acceptable collateral).

- Allowing the "holdback" of bond proceeds not supported by the required value-to-lien ratio until an MAI appraisal can demonstrate that the value-to-lien ratio has been achieved.

- Allowing for a second bond issuance.

Performing the RED Analysis™

As part of the Development Agreement negotiations, the jurisdictional staff will want to insert language into the Development Agreement indicating when specific infrastructure projects are to be completed. Many times, we have to construct this infrastructure up front in the development process in order to activate services to the community. Other times, we don't, and the request is solely driven by the jurisdiction's "wish" that the facility be constructed within a specific time period.

For instance, the jurisdiction may want a fire station constructed prior to residents moving in when the jurisdiction already has a fire station within service range. Alternatively, the jurisdiction may want the four-lane arterial roadway constructed the day the project opens; however, traffic counts will not require a four-lane arterial road for another ten years. While we don't disagree these improvements would be nice to have on opening day, they cost a tremendous amount of money, and deploying funds on infrastructure that is not required will negatively impact the financial returns and ultimate success of the project.

For these reasons, it is critical that we lay out what infrastructure our clients are responsible for and when such infrastructure will be constructed in the Development Agreement.

It's at this time that we perform the RED Analysis™, which stands for **R**educe, **E**liminate, and **D**efer. In other words, we take the time to simplify the project's infrastructure requirements without sacrificing any value.

In our example above, we request that the requirement to provide the fire station be eliminated as the existing fire facility will provide sufficient emergency service for the next ten years, at which point we can agree to purchase an additional piece of fire apparatus.

Additionally, we can request that our client only be required to construct the first two lanes of the arterial roadway until such point in time as the traffic counts dictate additional lanes are required. This is the essence of the RED Analysis: to review our client's construction costs and phasing schedule as we are negotiating with the jurisdiction to reduce, eliminate, or defer as much cash outflow in the initial phases of a project to revenue event. By pushing out these expenditures, we increase the project's financial returns, specifically the project's IRR.

Along the same lines, we have to be careful if the jurisdictional staff asks us to oversize utilities. If they do ask us to oversize elements of our infrastructure, my response will be strongly affirmative, as we want to be seen as working collaboratively with the jurisdiction; however, I make it clear we will only pay for our project's fair share. We will only fund what our project requires, so the jurisdiction will have to bring the incremental facility costs to the table if they want us to construct additional capacity in our project's water lines, sewer lines, water storage tanks, or anything else.

Given the option, try to avoid oversizing at all. There are a number of strategies you could employ to avoid it through the Development Agreement. The easiest and most straightforward means is to state that the developer will only be required to fund public improvements that are required by its projects using generally accepted engineering standards.

It probably won't surprise you to hear that every jurisdiction I have ever come across always says they have no money to assist in the provision of public improvements. Well, I'm here to say that these claims don't always line up with reality.

When we hear a jurisdictional representative say something along these lines, it's time to put on our green eye shades and dig into the jurisdiction's financial reports. Typically, when we start to go through the financial reports prepared by the jurisdiction's public accounting firm, we find unrestricted cash in specific accounts eligible for the jurisdiction to use toward offsetting infrastructure financing costs.

Once identified, we illustrate how the jurisdiction can either fully construct a facility and receive reimbursements over time with impact fees, hook-up fees, etc., or how the jurisdictions could fund their pro-rata share of public infrastructure costs in the case of an oversizing. When you bring up the fact that you found unrestricted cash balances in financing reports prepared in accordance with the Governmental Accounting Standards Board (GASB), the conversations get real interesting, real fast!

Financing Other Costs

In some areas of the county, we will create private impact fees for our land developer clients. We most often see this financing alternative in the Southwest. As this is a "private" agreement between the developer and the home builders, we don't need to include this in the Development Agreement, but rather, it is a clause we put into the purchase and sale agreement with the builder.

Effectively, this is nothing more than an increase in the lot price but is made to look, sound, and function like a jurisdictional impact fee. If you are going to do this, you need to make sure that the home builders are not paying both a "private" impact fee as well as a jurisdictional impact fee, as this could price your lots out of the market and jeopardize your project. I bring this up as it may be an option for your project.

Conversely, if our clients are building infrastructure for which the jurisdiction will collect impact fees, we need to work with them to determine whether they should consider passing impact fee credits on to the home builders. If they do, they can increase the residual land value of the builder lots and sell lots for a higher price. The other option is to collect the impact fee reimbursements over time. The client's response to The Return Factor Question will direct our thinking in relation to this issue. If the client is IRR driven, we recommend the credits be passed to the home builder, and if the client is Nominal Dollar driven, we recommend the collection of impact fees over time.

In some instances where a "private" impact fee is not an option but the jurisdiction has an impact fee program, we approach them with the request to establish a separate service area over our client's master planned community and charge a project-specific infrastructure impact fee. This will reimburse the client for the master planned community's eligible public facilities included in the Capital Improvement Program.

At this point, it is again important to remember our client's response to The Return Factor Question. If they responded that they were nominal dollar-driven, we would establish the Capital Improvement Program for the project's Service Area with infrastructure items that will <u>NOT</u> be financed with Special District bond proceeds. This way, we are collecting the largest amount of reimbursements over time. In essence, we are being reimbursed for one bucket of infrastructure costs through impact fees while simultaneously being reimbursed for another set of costs through the Special District, thereby achieving our client's goal of maximizing total reimbursements over time.

If our client is IRR-driven, this is not as important of a consideration. Please note that this is not a good option for smaller projects, as the jurisdiction will typically only do this if the project requires large-regional-serving infrastructure. Typically, projects need to be in excess of 1,000 acres to allow for the successful implementation of this financing strategy.

In the Development Agreement, we can also address reimbursement agreements. Are we building infrastructure others are benefiting from? If so, we can ask that the jurisdiction require other landowners who benefit from the infrastructure that we or the Special District are constructing to reimburse the payer for their pro-rata share of the cost of the facilities.

What about property tax increment? Does the jurisdiction provide the ability to collect property tax increment on the jurisdiction's property tax allocation? If so, we should negotiate with the jurisdiction to include this financing source in the Development Agreement.

Lastly, to the extent that we're generating construction sales tax, transaction privilege tax, leasing tax, or lodging tax, we want to make it possible for us to work with the jurisdiction to allow a portion of these funds to flow back to us.

This is the big-picture overview of just some of the financing vehicles we put in a Development Agreement. To summarize, when we are finished with the Development Agreement, we will have addressed and provided flexibility and certainty on a number of the Project D.O.S. issues initially discussed in the Project Vision, D.O.S. Conversation, and the Return Factor Question. More specifically, we will have accomplished the following:

- Determined which public improvement projects and other related costs (impact fees, engineering costs, legal costs, survey, staking, real property, financing costs, etc.) we can finance through the Special District(s).

- Documented the Special District's financing structure.

- Established what types of non-recourse, long-term, tax-exempt bonds can be used— SA Bonds, GO Bonds, or Revenue Bonds.

- Memorialized a target ad valorem tax rate (if using GO Bonds).

- Called out a required GO Bond Authorization amount (if using GO Bonds).

- Documented appraisal and assessment methodologies.

- Solved how to maximize the amount of funding "up front" when we need it the most.

- Finalized value-to-lien (if using SA Bonds).

- Outlined how the underwriter, bond counsel, appraiser, assessment engineer, and other Special District consultants will be selected.

- Performed the RED Analysis and outlined what types of public infrastructure will be constructed and when.

- Worked with the jurisdiction to create an impact fee Service Area to fund project-specific infrastructure.

- Outlined how other benefiting landowners will be funding their fair share of infrastructure costs through reimbursement agreements.

These financing components are not only important for Special District financing. All these elements work together, which is why it is crucial to have someone on your team who has seen and done it all. You should never assume everything will work out if you just issue a Special District bond or pay for some infrastructure.

Something could always go wrong, but more importantly, you're doing yourself a disservice. When you look closely at all of the moving parts, every challenge, and every opportunity, you can craft a robust financing strategy and document the same in the Development Agreement, which helps to de-risk the transaction and set yourself up for success.

One closing comment on drafting Development Agreements: it is essential to have very clear, very simple language in the Development Agreement. I can't stress this enough. When I say simple language, I mean so simple a monkey could understand it. Even then, I guarantee there can still be issues. We've been working with some very large projects now for nearly forty years, and every time a new jurisdictional attorney or jurisdictional manager comes in, they will read the Development Agreement while looking through their own lens. If the language is vague at all, they will interpret it in their own favor, not the developer's. The clearer and simpler your language can be, the better. Legalese is not your friend in these circumstances.

The other best practice we use in our Development Agreements is to include math computations. For instance, we will show how the fair share calculations should be done and also include footnotes as to where the data for the calculations is to be found. This serves the double purpose of assuring us we get the correct outcome while simultaneously providing clear instructions as to how the calculations are to be conducted in the future. It turns out it's much more difficult to willfully misinterpret math than words.

Takeaway: Load up your Development Agreement with favorable financing language, and make sure to include all financing methods using clear, simple language.

Prepare the District Petition and Formation Application

With the Development Agreement finished, we will need to establish the Special District. The application for forming a Special District looks very different depending on what state or jurisdiction you're in. It could involve filling in a few pages and providing a title report along with a legal description, or it could be an agonizingly long process involving hundreds of pages of information and narrative as supported by multiple exhibits.

When we prepare a district application, we make the most of the variable nature of these transactions. We customize our applications to outline the exact financing we planned and want to implement based on our Development Agreement. All these documents work together to play a role in the implementation of our financing.

I appreciate the district application as a formal record of the transaction. It clearly documents the intent of all parties involved when the district was formed. For example, we set up a district in the Southwest for a 9,770-acre master planned community, and we were trying to be very specific about what infrastructure we wanted to finance through the application in addition to the key deal points.

Twenty years into the project, we got a new jurisdictional attorney. They wanted to read into the Development Agreement and district financing agreement material that simply wasn't there. We couldn't have that! So, we were able to reference the application we had prepared twenty years previously and showed the intent of the parties. We pointed out what we applied for, what the jurisdiction had approved, and how we could finance any eligible public improvement by any type of bond we could issue pursuant to state statute. This little extra push helped us win the day.

This is another example of how all these documents tie together to tell a story, but someone needs to be there to tell it. We at Launch are committed to telling that story—making sure all the pieces of the project are well-connected, coherent, and consistent.

In a perfect world, I would lay out all critical terms in the Development Agreement. That way, once the Development Agreement is complete and we go on to petition the jurisdiction, we can tell the jurisdiction we've already agreed to all the salient points on the financing. They've been outlined in the Development Agreement, so there is nothing to negotiate, and we can move forward without delay.

Better yet, I often try to begin the district formation process on a parallel path with negotiating the Development Agreement. That way, once a project is annexed or approved, we are ready to establish the district while all of the deal points are fresh in everyone's mind. We can ensure nothing is lost in communication between when the Development Agreement is recorded and when the district is formed. I've seen the best results and the most clarity when we do both at the same time.

I can recall several cases where using this method, if it had been possible, would have saved a lot of grief. I had a client call me, asking if I would take a look at their Development Agreement. They were just about finished with it but wanted another opinion, particularly because they intended to form a Community Facilities District (CFD) in the state of Arizona.

I looked at it but immediately noticed it had no content in it related to the fact that the jurisdiction "will" establish the district. The language in the Development Agreement stated that when requested, the jurisdiction "may consider the establishment of the district." I also saw areas where more favorable language would be beneficial, especially relating to oversizing, development impact fee credits, and reimbursement agreements. I explained what I saw to the client and cautioned them not to proceed until the agreement was updated. Unfortunately, the client was in a hurry and decided to trust the jurisdiction. The client went ahead and recorded the Development Agreement.

Later, when we approached the jurisdiction with our preferred financing plan in the district application, the jurisdiction told us they would only create the district if we used general obligation bonds only. Our previous discussions with the jurisdiction included that we wanted to use special assessment bonds so that we could reduce our peak capital and lower our overall cost of capital. My client was stuck and ended up using a less-than-optimal financing structure for their project.

My client was taken advantage of just because they decided to trust the jurisdiction. It's always safer to have everything properly memorialized so there is no chance of misunderstanding or manipulation, intentional or not.

As part of the district application process, we insist on using the Development Agreement as a framework for the district's formation, double- and triple-checking that what we've planned is what is laid out in the district application.

Takeaway: Ensure the district formation application aligns precisely with the Development Agreement.

Coordinate the District Formation Process

Now that the application is submitted—what happens next? I've found that unless someone is proactively driving the process forward, nothing really happens. Between the jurisdiction, the district, and the myriad of consultants involved, it's not surprising to hear that delay is common, but it's never a desirable outcome.

To solve the issue, we have worked a whole step into The Launch Sequence dedicated to making things happen. As a result, we prepare a schedule of tasks, responsibilities, and due dates and hold people accountable to the schedule. This is a critical step to get the district formed in a timely manner.

I'm not telling anybody something they don't already know, but the best means to get any long-term project done is to have a standing call with a firm agenda. We work this standing call into everything we undertake. Again, it's not a groundbreaking strategy, but there is no better way to hold a team accountable and keep things rolling.

The next strategy we employ is to identify specific roles, tasks, and responsibilities and then match those to the people who represent them for the specific project. If something is moving slowly, it never hurts to get to the bottom of the issue by asking pointed questions:

- Whose responsibility is the task?

- Are they slipping, or are external circumstances a factor?

- Why are they slipping?

- What are they going to do to get caught up?

When we get to the bottom of these questions, it becomes easy to hold everyone accountable and keep the process moving forward.

Takeaway: Stay on top of forward progress by holding consistent meetings and identifying roles and responsibilities.

Review the Assessment Methodology (If Applicable)

Once we get the district formed, we start doing bond transactions, and the rubber hits the road. At this point, we're involving other consultants and getting ready to issue bonds for the construction or reimbursement of infrastructure.

As much as we would like to think that developers are in the bond-issuing business, they're not. They're in the lot-manufacturing business for home builders, who are in the business of providing homes to home buyers. It falls to us, then, to make sure that what we present to the home-buying public is something they want to buy.

In the Planning Phase, we discussed the importance of including amenities, topography, ingress, egress, and school districts in our plans. But what we at Launch take a close look at is the total effective property tax rate the home buyer is going to be purchasing as part of their principal, interest, taxes, and insurance (PITI). We will take that tax rate and compare it to the rest of the market.

When it comes to the preparation of assessment methodologies as it relates to the issuance of special assessment bonds, we want to make absolutely sure that when the assessment engineer prepares the final assessment methodology, the actual per-lot assessments correlate with the assessments we had planned for. If we had assumed a lot would be taking a $20,000 assessment, we would need to make sure the assessment engineers ended up with a $20,000 assessment on a per-lot basis.

The best way to ensure everything lines up in the end is to lay out the costs and how they are allocated to the benefiting property in the clearest way possible. Again, we'll often cover this in the Development Agreement. That way, we've already laid out the way in which benefits (e.g., costs) will be allocated to the individual lots and/or parcels. In other words, we have already done the math and provided everything necessary to get the $20,000 per-lot assessment.

This is so important because if we end up with a $15,000 per-lot assessment rather than $20,000, we will have left $5,000 per lot in unreimbursed costs on the table. If, on the other hand, we can push the assessment higher than what we had originally estimated, this just adds additional icing on the cake.

If we've done our Development Agreement homework well, we will even be able to select the assessment engineer to prepare the assessments in the manner we have laid out in the Development Agreement. Even if we are not working with an assessment engineer we know, we can still do the math ahead of time and give them the work product to review and double-check so we speed up the process as much as possible. They will usually make tweaks to make it their own, but we still generally get the number we want.

Takeaway: Make sure the assessment methodology is sound by matching up your calculations with reality.

Review Appraisal and Market Study

The next important component as it relates to assessment bonds is the review of the appraisal to ensure we're getting the valuation we think our finished lot is worth.

Attorneys are taught to never ask a question they don't already know the answer to. In the same way, we never lay down an assessment unless we know how the appraiser is going to value the land.

In many instances, we have access to the appraiser's financial models, so we can run the models and get an estimate of the fair market values that the appraiser will most likely determine. This is an important exercise as it informs our client and us what construction costs, phasing schedules, base home prices by lot segment, and absorption projections to provide to the appraiser.

If, for some reason, we run into an issue where the value does not come in as high as we had expected, it is usually because of a market correction, an increase in interest rates, or something else outside of our control. Even in that situation, however, we would have already included within the Development Agreement means by which we could issue the same amount of bonds we had originally estimated. Those mechanisms allow us to get the money we need even if we don't initially hit the value-to-lien requirements we had originally projected.

This is another example of why it is so important to understand value. Launch is unique because we are affiliated with the Land Advisors Organization, the largest land-only brokerage firm in the United States. The affiliation allows us access to the land sales comps in all the major markets. We know what everything is being placed on the market for, how long it is on the market, and what it is selling for. We know the value of the following:

- Raw land
- Entitled land
- Super pads
- Blue-top lots
- Finished lots

Additionally, we have a multitude of data sources to which we subscribe, which allows us to make sure our assumptions are reasonable and supportable to ensure we achieve our value estimates.

The appraisal is critical. Once we receive the appraisal back, we should know what it says because we've already put the work in, but we will go through it anyway to make sure all the numbers are ticking and tying. If, for any reason, our calculations and the appraiser's do not agree, we will always go back and start a new discussion about why we think the value should be something other than what is currently indicated.

This is the heart of implementation: we check and check again that everything is going according to plan, and any deviation is dealt with quickly and effectively. Even a small hitch can derail the entire plan, so attention to detail is absolutely critical.

Takeaway: Don't provide the appraiser with any project valuation assumptions unless you know what value the appraiser will arrive at using these assumptions.

Request Bond Issuance and Assist in the Preparation of the Official Statement

ow that we have our appraisal and assessment roll (created by our assessment methodology) in the case of an assessment bond, we can dive into bond issuance. With a GO Bond, we don't have to go through as much detailed analysis. The values we require to estimate our bond amounts are provided by the County Assessor's Office, and these figures are outside of Launch's and the developer's control.

Depending on the state and jurisdiction, we may have to prepare and present a formal financing request to the district or jurisdiction as dictated by statute. Once we have their approval, we can assemble the financing team, which includes the bond counsel, financial advisor, underwriter, underwriter counsel, disclosure counsel, and others as may be required (Financing Team).

The purpose of the Financing Team is to draft a Preliminary Offer Statement (POS) to provide to the municipal debt market as an invitation to purchase the bonds. Additionally, the Financing Team is also tasked with preparing all of the bond documents that are required as a part of the bond issue.

As part of the preparation of the POS, since we have been involved in the entire financing process since the Project Vision discussion, we assist the developer in preparing the narrative and supporting tables for the Developer and Project Description sections of the POS. Additionally, we will outline the improvements that will either be constructed or reimbursed as part of the bond financing.

Tracking infrastructure costs is an absolutely critical component of a Special District financing, as we have to demonstrate to the attorneys (and the SEC) that the tax-exempt bonds are being used for public infrastructure, the facilities were completed pursuant to plans and specs, and the facilities were paid for and accepted by the jurisdiction. Let me tell you, this is a lot of work, especially if you haven't done this before. This is why we invented the Launch Reimbursement System™ (LRS).[1]

---

[1]   http://www.launchlrs.com

The LRS is our cloud-based system used to track every eligible cost available for reimbursement through the district. This documentation collection is based on the state statutes in which the project is located; however, it typically includes the following:

- Prevailing wage reports (CA/NV)
- Public bidding reports
- Contracts
- Change orders
- Canceled checks / Proof of payment
- Lien releases
- Acceptance letters
- As-Built Plan Sets

If we know we're going to be issuing a bond and will have $15 million in bond proceeds to reimburse us for eligible infrastructure costs, we can go through the LRS checklist and select the items we want to be reimbursed until we reach a total of $15 million. We then hit a button, and the LRS assembles the selected project documents and electronically assembles the reimbursement packages for submission to the district for reimbursement.

The idea is to have everything laid out in advance so that the minute those bonds are issued, the $15 million comes into the district's project fund and gets wired out immediately to the developer.

Again, the LRS helps if we have had to prepare a request for financing. Because we have all of the costs and know how much money we can access for the next bond issuance, we don't even need to bother our clients with data requests. We just prepare the request, have our client approve it, and begin the bond issuance process all over again. As part of the POS process, we, for the most part, assist the developer in writing the development section. This will need to answer the following questions:

- Who is the developer?

- What is the experience of the developer?

- Who are the executive officers of the developer?

- How many similar projects has the developer completed to date?

- What is the description of the project in terms of acres?

- Is the project entitlement secured?

- Does it have access to water, sewer, and other services?

- Are additional permits or approvals required to be secured? Are there any lawsuits against the developer and/or project?

- What stage of development is the project in?

- How much has been expended to date?

- What is the status of the completion of facilities necessary to sell lots or homes?

- How many lots have been sold to builders?
- How many finished lots have been constructed?
- How many homes have been built and sold?
- How is the developer financing the project?
- What is the appraised value?

Essentially, this is a thorough examination of the development's status, entitlements, water and sewer sources, and other developmental considerations.

We'll also get into writing up the district, clarifying what bonds are being issued and what exactly we will be acquiring or constructing through that bond issuance. We typically handle this part because our clients are busy building. They have other considerations on their plates, and it ends up being faster and easier for us to take the initial swipe at it. When we give it back to the developer and their legal counsel, they can proof it, edit it, and otherwise make it their own document.

Again, our goal is to move this project forward smoothly and with the right answers for any problems that arise. We're entirely focused now on financing what was originally orchestrated during the Planning Process of The Launch Sequence.

Takeaway: Use the Launch Reimbursement System to keep track of all important costs as you are completing the official statement.

Review the Bond Documents for Clarity of Financial Matters

The final item related to the issuance of bonds is reading the mind-numbing documents associated with a bond issuance. The largest of these is the bond indenture. I cannot stress enough how important it is to scour the indenture to make sure it includes everything necessary to ensure that the transaction we planned and implemented is the transaction that is outlined in the indenture.

The indenture needs to include all the bells and whistles we included in the custom-crafted financing we put together during our Planning Process, as well as everything we wrote in the Development

Agreement, the district formation documents, and the request for bond issuance.

As I mentioned before, bond attorneys tend to print out the last deal they did with vague similarities to the current transaction, but that never works out. Because our transactions are custom-made, someone needs to go through the bond documents with a fine-toothed comb to ensure every detail is accurate and crystal clear in every matter related to finance.

So many of these documents fail to accurately reflect what was planned and implemented. The indenture is the guiding document for the financing, so if it is wrong, everything is wrong. Say we needed to go back in and fix the district for some reason. If we're lifting the hood on, it's going to be a shock to see that the engine is totally incompatible with the car. We need to know what engine we're installing and how that engine works.

I've never had to go back in and fix one of our districts, but we've intervened when others have had this exact issue with their indenture. It's messy and entirely preventable if you take this Implementation Process seriously.

Takeaway: Review the indenture. Then, check it again... and again.

PART 3
Lift Off

Next Steps

This takes us to the end of the Implementation Process. It truly is the most critical part of The Launch Sequence, and success or failure in activating this process seamlessly will go far in determining the ease with which things will progress in the long term.

This is where we memorialize and document the understanding of the parties—developer, jurisdiction, and district—as it relates to the development and financing of the project, which can take over fifty years to develop. As such, it is imperative that we create a document that creates certainty and flexibility to allow the developer to adjust their "financing sails" to meet the changing economic, market, and jurisdictional winds they will encounter over the years.

If you follow the steps of the Implementation Process, you will be well-equipped to create clear, concise, thoughtful documents that anticipate all potential opportunities and challenges that may occur during the development of the project. Even better, you will have included language in the development and financing agreements to anticipate these items so that the parties never need to "open up" and amend the agreements. When this happens, it inevitably costs the developer hundreds of thousands—if not millions—of dollars.

At this point, we have formed the district and issued the first series of bonds. The bond proceeds are now flowing back to the trustee and being held for distribution to the developer. Now, all the consultants leave, and the developer and district staff are left to look at each other and ask, "Now what?"

The short answer is the Management Process.

In the next book, we will explore how to manage your master planned community in such a way that the only thing left for you to do is sit back and "Manage Your Fortune."

Afterword

As you have learned more about how the Implementation Process works, we hope you feel inspired to take advantage of the simplicity and clarity of The Launch Sequence. Maybe you see echoes of your own master planned community dreams in these pages of success stories.

Most likely, though, your set of dangers, opportunities, and strengths is different from anything you've heard about here. That is even more exciting! Every project is unique, and we would love to come up with new ways to leverage your D.O.S. and help you implement your plans.

Regardless of where you are in your project, Launch is ready for you.

Scan the QR Code below to Access Supplemental Documents and Book Bonuses

About the Author

Carter is an author and the Managing Principal of Launch Development Finance Advisors. Prior to the founding of Launch, Carter was the Co-Founder and Managing Principal of Development Planning and Financing Group. Preceding this, Carter was a Manager in the real estate consulting department of the national accounting firm of Kenneth Leventhal & Company in both the Phoenix, Arizona, and Newport Beach, California offices. Carter is a Certified Public Accountant in Arizona, California, and Texas, as well as a former State Certified Real Estate Appraiser in Arizona. He holds a master's degree in Real Estate

Development from the University of Southern California and a bachelor's degree in Business Economics from the University of California, Santa Barbara.

With over forty years of experience in the real estate consulting industry, Carter's area of specialty is in the formulation and implementation of land-secured financings for large-scale developments and the formulation of development strategies for large-scale master-planned communities.

Carter served as a City of Phoenix's Camelback Village Planning Committee member. He is a full member of the Urban Land Institute, Valley Partnership, and is a member of numerous Building Industry Associations in Arizona, California, Idaho, and Texas. Carter authored the 2008 and 2016 National Association of Home Builders' Impact Fee Handbook as well as the 2025 Impact Fee Update.

Enjoy The Other Books in the Land To Lots Series

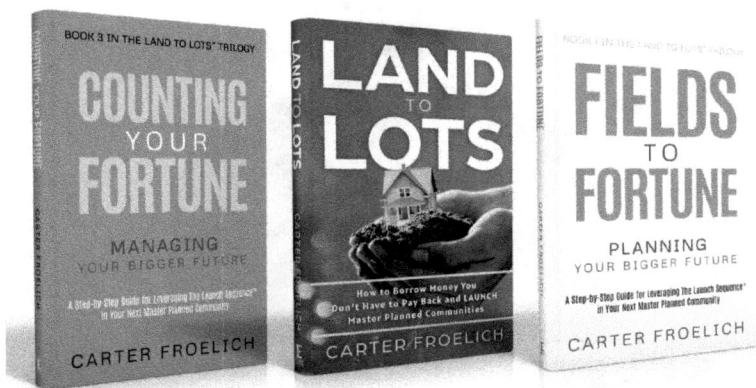

COUNTING YOUR FORTUNE
BOOK 3 IN THE LAND TO LOTS™ TRILOGY
MANAGING YOUR BIGGER FUTURE
A Step-by-Step Guide for Leveraging The Launch Sequence™ in Your Next Master Planned Community
CARTER FROELICH

LAND TO LOTS
How to Borrow Money You Don't Have to Pay Back and LAUNCH Master Planned Communities
CARTER FROELICH

FIELDS TO FORTUNE
BOOK 1 IN THE LAND TO LOTS™ TRILOGY
PLANNING YOUR BIGGER FUTURE
A Step-by-Step Guide for Leveraging The Launch Sequence™ in Your Next Master Planned Community
CARTER FROELICH

AVAILABLE WHEREVER BOOKS ARE SOLD

LAND TO LOTS® PODCAST

LAND TO LOTS®
ACQUISITION, DEVELOPMENT & FINANCE

Carter Froelich hosts the Land to Lots® podcast where he and his team help their clients finance infrastructure, reduce costs and mitigate risks all with the goal of enhancing project profitability.

LANDTOLOTS.COM

THIS BOOK IS PROTECTED INTELLECTUAL PROPERTY

Instant IP ™

The author of this book values Intellectual Property and has utilized Instant IP, a groundbreaking technology.
Instant IP is the patented, blockchain-based solution for Intellectual Property protection.

Blockchain is a distributed public digital record that can not be edited. Instant IP timestamps the author's ideas, creating a smart contract, thus an immutable digital asset that proves ownership and establishes a first to use / first to file event.

Protected by Instant IP ™

LEARN MORE AT INSTANTIP.TODAY

www.ingramcontent.com/pod-product-compliance
Lightning Source LLC
Chambersburg PA
CBHW071440210326
41597CB00020B/3875